YOU CAN BIKE ACROSS AMERICA
A GUIDE TO BIKING ACROSS THE UNITED STATES SELF-SUPPORTED

This book and all contents herein may not be copied or distributed without the author's explicit, written permission except in the case of brief quotes and excerpts used for review. All rights reserved.

© 2017 by Isaiah Rain Maynard

For all inquiries, please e-mail
youcanbikeacrossamerica@gmail.com

Printed in the United States of America

First Printing, April of 2017

ISBN 13: 978-1540447838
ISBN-10: 1540447839

www.youcanbikeacrossamerica.com

Cover design and Illustrations
By Isaiah Rain Maynard
© Isaiah Rain Maynard
www.isaiahrainmaynard.com

YOU CAN BIKE ACROSS AMERICA
A GUIDE TO BIKING ACROSS THE UNITED STATES SELF-SUPPORTED

ISAIAH RAIN MAYNARD

TABLE OF CONTENTS

- 1 **SECTION ONE** INTRODUCTION
  - 2   INTRODUCTION
  - 4   WHO AM I?

- 7 **SECTION TWO** BEFORE THE RIDE
  - 8   CHAPTER 01 QUESTIONS TO ASK YOURSELF
  - 12   CHAPTER 02 ROUTES
    - 12   PLANNING
    - 13   ADVENTURE CYCLING ASSOCIATION
    - 14   MAPS
    - 16   SHIPPING A BIKE
    - 16   ROADS
  - 21   CHAPTER 03 COSTS
    - 21   ESTIMATE YOUR COST

- 25 **SECTION THREE** GEAR
  - 26   CHAPTER 04 YOUR BIKE
    - 26   SIZING
    - 27   FRAMES
    - 27   BRAKES
    - 28   SHIFTING
    - 29   HANDLEBARS
    - 30   PACKING
    - 31   PANNIERS
    - 31   TRAILERS
    - 32   HANDLEBAR BAG
    - 33   LOADED BIKE
    - 34   UPGRADES
    - 35   BIKE SEAT
    - 36   BIKE LIGHTS
  - 38   CHAPTER 05 CAMPING
    - 39   CAMPING
    - 40   COOKING
  - 42   CHAPTER 06 TOOLS AND EXTRA
    - 42   BIKE TOOLS
    - 43   PATCH KITS
  - 45   CHAPTER 07 APPAREL
    - 46   BIKING APPAREL
    - 47   FOUL WEATHER GEAR

- 48 **SECTION FOUR** ON BIKING
  - 49   CHAPTER 08 SAFETY
    - 49   LOADED BIKES

50	SHOULDERS
51	REFLECTORS
52	**CHAPTER 09 EFFICIENCY**
52	TYPICAL DAY
53	CADENCE
54	WIND
54	TERRAIN
55	RESTING
56	CENTENNIAL RIDES
58	**CHAPTER 10 CLIMBING PASSES**
59	TIPS
59	ENTERTAINMENT
60	GEARS
61	**CHAPTER 11 TOWNS**
61	POST OFFICES
62	BIKE SHOPS
62	GROCERY STORES
62	HOSTELS
64	**CHAPTER 12 EATING AND HYDRATION**
64	FILTRATION
65	GETTING FOOD
66	MEALS
67	**CHAPTER 13 ON SLEEPING**
67	FIND A PLACE TO SLEEP
71	**CHAPTER 14 REPAIRS**
72	FLATS
72	CHAINS
73	SPOKES

74	**SECTION FIVE** RESOURCES & FAQ
75	**CHAPTER 15 RESOURCES**
75	MAPS
77	GEAR LIST
78	BIKE RECOMMENDATIONS
79	**CHAPTER 16 F. A. Q.**
79	F.A.Q.
89	THE FATE OF PUBLIC LANDS
91	PHOTOS

DISCLAIMER:
ALTHOUGH I PROVIDE RECOMMENDATIONS THROUGHOUT THIS BOOK, IT IS ULTIMATELY UP TO YOU TO BE SAFE AND PLAN ACCORDINGLY FOR YOUR TRIP. DUE TO THE NATURE OF THIS GUIDE-BOOK, I AM NOT AND WILL NOT BE RESPONSIBLE FOR ANY MISHAPS OR INJURIES YOU INCUR, SHOULD YOU SET OUT TO TACKLE THE UNITED STATES BY BICYCLE. GOOD JUDGMENT AND PHYSICAL CAPABILITIES ARE YOUR CALL. GOOD LUCK, HAVE FUN, AND BE SAFE!

THIS BOOK IS DEDICATED TO ALL THE SOULS OUT THERE THAT STAY TRUE TO THEMSELVES AND PERSEVERE, REGARDLESS OF OTHER PEOPLE'S DOUBTS AND LIMITING BELIEFS. FOR IT IS THESE INDIVIDUALS THAT WILL GUIDE THE WAY FOR EVERYONE IN TIMES OF NEED.

INTRODUCTION

SECTION **ONE**
INTRODUCTION

INTRODUCTION

Are you thinking about doing a self-supported bike tour, but don't know where to start? I know your answer is at least a partial yes, and that is why I am so happy that you have picked up this book.

Deciding to ride a bicycle across the United States is an endeavor that many dream about, but few live out. I have met many people that say, "I've always wanted to do that, but never will," or they tell me, "I'm too old". It makes me sad, because I know from personal experience that anyone can do it, regardless of circumstance.

I've been in Minnesota and shared lunch on the side of the road with a 76 year old, biking across the United States for the fifth time! My parents biked across the country with a two year old in a burley wagon. I've seen single women riding coast to coast. I have shared centennial rides with a couple on their honey-moon. A man with one leg biked across the United States[1]! I have seen a range of cyclists who manifest this dream and I can tell you that *you* are entirely capable!

I truly believe bike-touring is one of the greatest forms of travel available in the modern world, and I think everyone who has an ounce of adventure in their heart should set out on their

---

1   David Keifer has biked across the United States multiple times, participating in RAAM. See page 77 for article link.

own tour, at least once in this life.

At the time that I am writing this, it has been two years since I completed my ride (more on this later), and I still love talking about it and inspiring other's to adopt this form of travel and adventure. I have received a lot of questions since then about how to successfully do a bike tour, and the planning that goes into it. This book is the answer to all questions asked, and those that have yet to be asked. I wrote it with all levels of bike-tourers in mind; from people who have never packed so much as a backpack and rode a few miles, to people who may bike 500 miles a week but have never thought of spending a few weeks on a tour, even to those who may ride annually—but are looking to expand their knowledge in the topic of touring.

From planning to biking, I will take you through every step of the journey that is bike-touring, and hopefully it will inspire and empower you to pack your life into some panniers, and set out on the open road! I truly believe that bike-touring can not only be done by anyone... it *should* be done by everyone!

Prior to my ride, I spent countless hours online researching how to ride a bike across the United States, learning as much as I could. The problem was there seemed to be no compact collection of information on the topic--that's where this book comes in. *You Can Bike Across America* is drawn not only from all of the information I had collected in preparation, but also my direct experience with a self-supported bike ride across the United States. I believe that if you have found this, you will find it very helpful.

Thank you, and enjoy!

WHO AM I?

You may be wondering who I am, and what business I have creating a book on the subject of riding a bicycle across the United States. So, before we begin, let me tell you about myself and share how I found out about this wonderful form of travel.

I grew up in Steamboat Springs, Colorado. Tucked away in Northwest Colorado, there are endless forms of recreation available. Retrospectively, I can see how growing up in a mountain-town instilled within me the yearning for exploration and self discovery. It was a relationship that I had enjoyed, yet misunderstood until I began high school on the small island of Martha's Vineyard. High school was an interesting period for me as I struggled to find true purpose in the work that was school. There was an aspect of the self that seemed to be missing. I got a glimpse of that self during my participation on the Varsity Cross Country team. It was here, in the foot race, where I found the crossroads of body and mind. A delicate dance between strength and fatigue, hope and submission. It was rewarding to face difficulty and exhaustion with a toned mind, and overcome doubt. From my first race on, I searched for ways to develop my mind, and create within it the tapes of success.

In 2013, I was finishing up my Junior year of high school and I decided that as soon as I graduated in the following spring I was going to ride a bicycle across the United States. It seemed

INTRODUCTION

to be an excellent platform to put my mind and body to the test. So began an unbelievably rewarding journey. Having made a true decision—a real commitment—to something outside of my comfort zone, I began to grow immensely as an individual through a constant effort to become the cyclist I wasn't.

My mom and dad had each biked across the country together when they were raising my older brother, and I had grown up hearing about the time they spent on bikes while we flipped through their photo journals. However, I had never spent too much time biking myself. As I began to explore this new dream and formulate a plan to do it, I was able to turn to them for support. Needless to say, my parents were on-board with my plans and encouraged me to follow through. For that, I am thankful—I was fortunate enough to have parents willing to let their 18 year old son ride a bike 3,800 miles alone for a summer.

The excitement of my ensuing bike ride carried me through my final year of school. I spent as much of my free time as possible researching routes, reading blogs, talking to people who had done it, and watching hours of YouTube videos of cyclists from around the world. I consumed as much information about their trips as I could, not due to figuring out logistics, but simply because it got me excited about my own trip! It is worth noting that during this phase of my life, I was deeply invested in personal development. Along with reading about biking, I was assimilating content that was sculpting my mind. It would become clear to me that I had to ride not as the man I was, but rather as the man I was becoming.

As the year came to a close, I had purchased my bike—a Trek 520—collected all the necessary gear, aligned myself with a non profit, built a website with a blog, collected donations and sponsorships from some local businesses as well as from generous friends and family—even strangers. Two days after my graduation ceremony I was on a plane from Boston to Seattle, to rendezvous with my mom and pick up my bike from a FedEx center. Shortly thereafter, I had began biking out of Oak Harbor, Washington to begin my first ever bike tour; a coast to coast ride across the Northern portion of the United States, alone.

    This trip had a profound effect on who I am today. It gave me a gift, and I feel it is my honor to share that gift with others. Bicycle touring gives the cyclist the gift of the present moment. It requires attention to one place, in one moment. On the bike there are two wheels, one of which is essentially rolling into the future while the other is rolling out the past. It is precisely between these wheels where you are perched to explore, and drive. Throughout a bike tour you can experience life in its truest form, facing challenges and obstacles with zeal for the opportunity you are living.

BEFORE THE RIDE

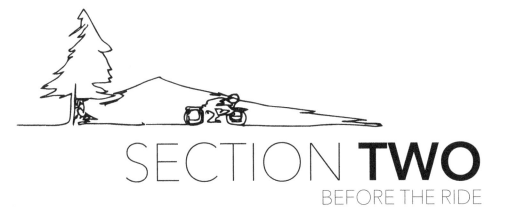

SECTION **TWO**
BEFORE THE RIDE

QUESTIONS TO ASK YOURSELF

Before you begin planning your tour, I suggest asking yourself these questions. They will be helpful in narrowing down your tour's details, which will make planning more effective. It is important to note that these questions, and the rest of the content in this book will be catered to people who intend to ride across the country without the aid of additional support; we call this a self-supported trip. You will be carrying all of the things you will need on your bicycle—that's right, no vans and no one to haul your things over the passes—just you, your bike and the will power to continue.

QUESTIONS

WHY HAVE YOU DEVELOPED AN INTEREST IN BIKE TOURING?

Bike touring is arguably the greatest way to see the country! When you are on a tour, you are in the open air—the landscape becomes part of the experience in a way that a car will never allow. It is precisely this reason that makes bike touring the greatest mode of transportation and adventure. It is an extremely empowering feeling to propel yourself thousands of miles with your own body and the aid of a machine. Bike touring also allows the individual to travel at their own desired pace, with the mobility and flexibility to explore wherever they please.

WOULD YOU BIKE ALONE, OR WITH A PARTNER OR A GROUP?

Although there are advantages to biking with a group, there are also advantages to biking alone. Ultimately, the biggest advantage goes to the solo-cyclist since they can control the most important aspect of the ride—pace.

Are you the type of person who likes to be spontaneous and not adhere to a specific schedule? If so, either make sure your partner shares the same traits and interests as you, or when you have the option to turn in after 30 miles because a town strikes your fancy but your partner would rather continue on—you're going to have some things to settle.

I was thankful that I was the only one in charge of my pace. It allowed to me spend extra time in places I found interesting, and blow through places that didn't appeal to me.

HOW MUCH TIME DO YOU HAVE TO TOUR?

This is an important question to answer since it dictates where and for how long you can be on a tour. If you only have two weeks, you may be better off staying close to home. If, on the other hand, you've thrown in the towel for that lame, soul-sucking office job and you have untold days of freedom—set off to tackle a continent! No matter how small or large in scale, a bike tour is an incredible experience.

If you really want to ride across the country, plan for about two to three and a half months. More on that in the next section, though.

DO YOU LIKE TO CAMP, OR DO YOU PREFER A HOTEL?

I love to camp—many times I prefer to sleep outside even when I have the option to be in my house. For this reason, the reality of being able to bike outside all day, and then find a place of my own to pitch a tent every night for two months straight was almost a dream come true.

Most people could go either way, but I have met people who "refuse" to camp—they will have a hard time finding a place to stay in, say, the middle of Montana on a back road. It can be done though, through a humble network of motels and careful mileage planning. However, if you love to camp, finding a place to stay every night becomes a simple task—by allowing flexibility.

ARE YOU UP FOR A MENTAL CHALLENGE, AS WELL A PHYSICAL CHALLENGE?

I may not have met you, but I know something about you. I know that you have an interest in bike touring. Whether or not you are already addicted, haven't even gone for an overnight, or just like to hear about it—you're interested. This interest, if cultivated correctly, can grow into something more.

Riding a bicycle across the United States sounds like a physical feat that will challenge anyone. I am not here to tell you that is easy, or that it is difficult. I am simply here to say, quite simply, it is a challenge. A challenge that has overwhelming payoff if it is faced. You need to be willing to face the challenges with an open mind and steadfast focus. Mentally, this sort of trip can break you—but in those moments you are put back together stronger than ever.

DO YOU BELIEVE YOU CAN DO IT?

If your answer is yes, you have the single most important factor out of the way. You really only need a bike now. You see, having faith in your ability to complete this task is essential. It is here, in your own self confidence where you can find the strength to continue when you're utterly exhausted. It is here where there is a voice reminding you why you started all those miles ago.

ROUTES

So hopefully by now you have nailed down whether or not you are traveling alone or with some partners. You should also know how much time you can allow to spend on the road. Additionally, you should have a firm belief in yourself that you are entirely capable of completing this trip.

PLANNING YOUR ROUTE

This is your chance to see the country on a bike! Are there any specific places you'd like to see? For example, I knew I wanted to start in Port Townsend, Washington and end on Martha's Vineyard in Massachusetts, while being able to see Glacier National Park, the Mississippi River, family in Wisconsin, and the Great Lakes. So It wouldn't make sense for me to bike a Southern Route, right? Right. Biking across the country is a feat in itself, but it is about the places that you see along the way, and the people you meet more so than going coast to coast.

As for making those dreams a reality, you will need a route to bike that is safe and efficient. There is no better resource to turn to than the Adventure Cycling Association (ACA). They make maps for touring cyclists, and can save you hours of headaches.

ADVENTURE CYCLING ASSOCIATION

The ACA is truly a gift to cyclists around the world. From their "About Us" page on their website (adventurecycling.org).

"As a nonprofit organization, Adventure Cycling Association's mission is to inspire and empower people to travel by bicycle. Established in 1973 as Bikecentennial, we are the premier bicycle-travel organization in North America with more than 35 years of experience and 50,000 members… We research and produce cycling maps for the Adventure Cycling Route Network, one of the largest cycling route networks in the world at 45,003 miles and growing. We are also the lead organization working to create an official U.S. cycling route network, the U.S. Bicycle Route System. Once complete, it will be the largest official cycling route network on the planet."

THEIR MAPS

Out of the 45,003 miles they have mapped and deemed safe for bike travel, they offer three routes that will take you coast to coast. In addition to that, they have 22 other routes within the states that be used in tandem with your coast to coast ride.

Take a look at the maps that they have available, there is a link below this section. I would explore all the options they have, specifically the Northern Tier, Southern Tier and Trans America Trail.

Not only are their maps accurate and efficient, they are very detailed and contain information that is useful to the touring cyclist. Such as hostels, detour information, cool sights, things to avoid, terrain and topography for the day ahead and even more! During my ride, I would say that 75 percent of all other cyclists I encountered were using ACA maps, and loving them.

Here are their maps!: (Broken up to show correct typing)
www.adventurecycling.org
/routes-and-maps/adventure-cycling-route-network
/interactive-network-map/

Their maps are not the only option though, and I myself ultimately ended up using a combination of Google Maps and State Maps, which I will explain next.

GOOGLE MAPS

You can effectively navigate your way coast to coast using only Google Maps, and it is entirely free (under the condition that your phone has data or you have Internet access). During my trip, I used Google Maps almost daily and found it most useful for being able to predict what kind of terrain I would be biking—using its elevation feature (explained on page 19). I also found it great for viewing towns before I got to them, a luxury that cyclists didn't have 15 years ago. By doing this, I could scan for places to camp like baseball dugouts, parks or campgrounds. A few times I even used it to see how long certain roads were gravel in Montana and North Dakota, saving my tires.

STATE MAPS

The truth is, Google Maps just lacks too many things for me to use it as stand alone navigation. For example, it doesn't provide a physical archive of my ride like my state maps do. I would buy my state maps when I saw the first gas station in whatever state

I was entering. I would then proceed to draw a marker line over every mile of road that I biked, leaving notes along the way such as mileage, memories, flat ties, etc. Now I have a set of 13 maps that all have a piece of history on them.

Another reason state maps are great is that they work all the time because they are on paper. So if your phone dies, you can still navigate. Having a state map shows every possible road to bike on, has very detailed information about town size, city size, secondary highways, interstates, places to stop and scenic views. However, they are not specific to the cyclist like ACA maps, so you can miss out on important information (why I used Google Maps in tandem). Left out information would include bike shop locations, hostels, water fill ups... Things like that.

They aren't free like Google either, but for $11-15 bucks a pop, they are well worth it.

WEST TO EAST OR EAST TO WEST

No matter what source you choose to navigate during your ride, it is ultimately up to you to decide which coast to start on. I personally recommend starting on the West Coast (Pacific) and ending on the East Coast (Atlantic), for two reasons:

1. In general, weather and wind moves West to East. Any cyclist knows that wind can make or break your day. You don't want to end up in Montana battling a head wind trying to get to the West Coast and wishing you were going the other way! I can personally recall many faces of disenfranchised cyclists gritting their teeth into the wind, while I relayed an ear-to-ear grin coasting in my tailwind. That is not to say that I didn't have my fair share of brutal head winds on my route though.

2. You bike the mountain passes first. Personally, I would

recommend biking mountain passes at the beginning of your trip because it gets you in shape, physically and mentally. Once you get to the East Coast, you will be strong and capable of tackling the endless rolling hills and valleys. I was relieved when I finished my last pass and knew nothing would near the scale of the Rockies for the next 30 or so days!

However, this is your own tour, and you can do what you want.

SHIPPING YOUR BIKE

Even if you live on the East Coast and want to start on the West Coast, you can do that! In fact, that is exactly what I did! There is an awesome company out there called Bike Flights® that works in partnership with FedEx to ship bikes at an affordable cost. You can find more information about Bike Flights at *bikeflights.com*. Do not let the coast you live closest to determine your starting location, unless you want it to.

ROADS

The United States has a diverse system of roads, many of which are great for biking and some that are worth avoiding. Let's go over them;

Interstates –Biking on Interstates is only legal in Montana and North Dakota, and even then, I would stay off of them. It's too noisy and the cars move really fast. Then there is also the fact that interstates just aren't as beautiful as the winding secondary highways.

State Highways – Unless it's a highway Michigan, you will find these roads to be smooth, have an adequate shoulder, and they tend to be a straight shot through towns. They are the most ideal road for touring, in my opinion.

What's the deal with Michigan? Of all the roads I encountered, none were as bad as any road I pedaled on in Michigan. From three inch cracks, to varying top-fills, broken up shoulders and rocky tar, they were flat-out nasty. If you are going to bike through Michigan, make sure you have extra tubes—and patience. However, do not let that deter you from biking through Michigan, as it is beautiful and a unique part of the country to see.

County Roads— I often would take a back road simply because it looked nice to ride on. Sometimes they are dirt, which can be undesirable. Shoulders on these roads are smaller than state highways, but with less traffic than the highways, they are pristine for riding!

Bike Paths — There are many states that have excellent networks of bike paths. There are even states that have converted railroads into bike paths, which were my favorite thing to bike on, they are beautiful. Thankfully, an organization exists that has cataloged all of the converted bike paths in the country. That organization is called Rails to Trails Conservancy. From their website's "About Us" page:

Rails to Trails Conservancy(RTC) serves as the national voice for more than 160,000 members and supporters, 31,000 miles of rail-trails and multi-use trails, and more than 8,000 miles of potential trails waiting to be built, with a goal of creating more walkable, bikeable communities in America.

Every day I would look at my route, and then cross reference to see if any RTC trails were available. They are beautiful trails and often take you along a way you would otherwise never travel.

REAL TIME CHANGES

No matter how specific you get with your planning, you'll never be able to predict real time changes. Such things may include road construction, detours, impassable roads due to conditions, or even bike problems. This is why planning can only go so far with an adventure of this scale. So, plan for flexibility more than anything else.

COMMON ROAD SIGNS TO KNOW

There are many signs that you will come across while biking across the United States. Here I have laid out the most important ones for you to know and understand.

You may be wondering why a gas marker is pictured; it is because gas means a place to fill up your water bottles! By far the most beneficial marker for a cyclist is the graded hill marker, you will find that the sight of one of these is enough to make your day.

BEFORE THE RIDE

USING GOOGLE MAPS

Once I actually started my trip, I found it more useful to plan my route on a day-to-day basis. So each night I would take out my state map and take a look at the next 100 or so miles, and then plan where to end. Like mentioned earlier, I primarily used the service for scouting what the day's elevation terrain looked like, and for looking at towns.

ROUTE ELEVATION

1. Pick your start and end locations. For this example, I am using my trips total route, starting in Port Townsend, Washington and ending on the island of Martha's Vineyard, in Massachusetts. The process is the same for town to town.

2. Google will spit out a small report (on right) telling you estimated total mileage, as well as an elevation profile. Notice how it goes gradually *dowhill*--West to East? Additionally, it will show you your route between destinations (below).

SCOUTING TOWNS

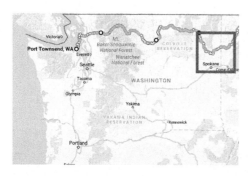

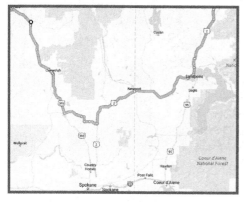

Taking a look at the first state I rode through, we can see the route goes the whole length of the state. We can also observe that it is not taking any major highways.

The border into Idaho is an important section to look at (in bold). To avoid crossing into Idaho on an interstate, in this case I-90, I needed to take Route 2 up into Newport. It is important to look at these border crossings in each state to ensure that you can make it safely, and with minimal backtracking.

Taking Route 2 was perfect for me anyway, because I was staying with family friends in Sandpoint.

PICKING A TOWN TO SLEEP IN

Imagine you can either bike to a town 85 miles away, or 94 miles away. How do you decide which one is a better option? I used Google Maps to make these decisions often.

To compare them, visit Google Maps and look at each of the towns on satellite mode. Now simply compare amenities, look for public parks, campgrounds, dugouts, whatever you want! This information will help make your decision. Additionally, asking any local in the area will often be more useful than Google itself. Imagine that, people more useful than technology!

BEFORE THE RIDE

COSTS

HOW MUCH DOES BIKING ACROSS THE UNITED STATES COST?

Prior to my ride, this was my most important question to answer. After all, you can't fund a bike tour without money. In this section I break down–in real numbers–the cost of my bike tour, and share insights into how you can effectively plan the cost of your own.

MY STATS

I spent exactly 48 days on tour, and my ride cost me right around $3,200.00. That was including the cost of all my gear (bike included), food, motels, camp fees, as well as miscellaneous expenses. For a breakdown of the exact gear you will need for a tour, refer to page 78.

ESTIMATING YOUR COSTS

The largest expense for a bike tour is most likely going to

be purchasing a bike, closely followed by food you will eat on tour (if you're like me, plan for four square meals a day). The good news is, you may already have a bike that is ready to take on tour! To find out, go to page 26. As for determining the cost of your tour, there are a few things we will need to consider, such as:

1. Roughly how many days you will be biking
2. What gear you still need
3. What you spend daily on food
4. Factor in additional miscellaneous costs

1. HOW MANY DAYS WILL YOU BE BIKING?

This can be answered using some simple math. Look at your Google estimate for miles, and then divide it by a conservative daily mileage. This will vary greatly between people, but a good rule of thumb is to average 12 miles an hour for the day. Then decide how many hours a day you'd bike. I figured if I averaged seven hours biking at 12 miles an hour I could knock out 84 miles. Then I rounded *down* just to be safe.

*Your Google estimate is your start and end location, plugged into Google Maps. My example is on page 19.

Here is an example:

Total mileage estimate: 3,800 / 80 Miles a day = 47.5 days
You may estimate a daily mileage of 60 miles, or even 100. Just be conservative in your planning, depending on your ability.
From there, factor in some days where you wouldn't bike (Rest Days)—seven seems reasonable. So now you are ball-parking a 55 day trip.

2. FACTOR IN THE GEAR THAT YOU STILL NEED

Depending on what you already have, you may not need to spend much more money. Refer to my gear checklist on page 77 of this book to see exactly what you will need for this trip.

Total needed for gear: $_____

3. HOW MUCH WILL YOU SPEND ON FOOD

Now, think about a typical day and how much money you spend on food. This is ultimately your only true and constant expense on a bike tour, unless you plan on sleeping in a motel every night.

I figured that I could survive on about $20 a day. This would look like, $20 x 55 = $1100. It is important to round up here, because you don't want to under-budget. In the end, I spent just under $20 a day on average.

How much will you plan to spend on food a day?: $_____

4. ADDITIONAL COSTS

I thought it would be smart to budget another $200 for any kind of emergency purchase. This would include extra tubes, bike chain repairs, new clothes… you know, the unpredictable–but predictable–things!

I ended spending this $200 on things like shipping fees when I mailed home extra weight, gifts for friends, a new chain, a new rear tire as well as memorabilia from neat places. The amount you'll bring will vary depending on your purchasing habits.

Total needed for miscellaneous purchases: $_____

    Now you can total up the costs, and that is what you should plan to have available for your trip. It is important to note that this is an estimation, and you may find that one month in, you spend a lot more, or a lot less than anticipated. That is why I advise you to "over budget".

    Total: $_____

MONEY FOR ALL YOUR GEAR!

SECTION THREE
GEAR

YOUR BIKE

BIKE 101

The most important piece of gear that you will need for your cross country tour will be a bike. If you already have a bike, chances are you could ride it across the country—no matter what kind it is! I have personally seen people crossing the country on beach cruisers, unicycles, and tandem bikes (with one or two riders!)

However, to make things more enjoyable for you, I suggest that you look into the following information:

FRAME SIZE

If your bike does not fit properly, you're going to have a bad time. To ensure that your bike does fit properly, you'll want to go to your local bike shop and get fitted. There are many resources available online but nothing comes close to the effectiveness of a true fit in person with the bike you will be riding every day.

I am 5' 6" and ride a 54cm frame, you may be 5' 6" and *not* ride a 54cm frame, due to body geometry. **Do not overlook fit!**

STEEL FRAME

Steel is the best frame material, which may seem counter-intuitive due to its weight. However, steel has certain properties that make it ideal for biking. For one, it dampens vibrations much more efficiently than aluminum. This may sound like a wash, but if you think about the hours you will spend on your bike, you may understand why having less bone-rattling vibration will be better. Secondly, it is weldable, which can save you if you get in trouble and bust your frame (yes, I have heard of it happening).

27 SPEED MINIMUM

This is just a recommended number, and the same speed configuration of my bike (Trek 520). Speeds are found by multiplying the number of gear rings on your front cog by the number of rings on your rear cog. So, mine was a 3 x 9 set. A lot of bikes will come standard with 18 speeds (2 x 9), which is fine—but if you have the option, get more speeds because they truly come in handy when you are climbing passes or cranking out a high-mileage day. It will also be easier on your legs. The benefit of a 3 x 9 set is you get to use a granny-gear. Granny gear is the lowest gear on a bicycle. So, by having a 3 x 9 instead of a 2 x 9 you will have a lower gear ratio, making climbing even easier.

BRAKES

There are two main types of brakes that you'll find on a bike; disk and cantilever. For touring, you really cannot go wrong with either. Disk brakes are more responsive and the braking ability is superior compared to cantilever.

The advantage of a cantilever brake is their mechanical simplicity—something that should not be overlooked when bike touring. It is a lot easier to MacGyver a cantilever brake in the middle of nowhere than it is with a disk brake. The only issue with a ride of this scale is that with a cantilever brake the cable will likely begin to stretch from tension. This is a simple fix.

BAR END SHIFTERS VS STI

Typically, in today's bike market you're going to find two options for shifting. Bar end shifters, and Shimano Total Integration (STI) shifters. The main difference between the two is the mechanics.

I personally prefer and recommend getting Bar End Shifters because they are more reliable and durable. Additionally, they are easier and less expensive to fix if something were to go wrong, like your bike falling over. (If you have STI shifters and your bike falls over, you're practically KO'd.)

It is worth noting here that there is another type of shifting mechanism, called frame shifting, that can be found time to time on older bikes. The mechanics of this are virtually identical to that of bar end shifters, but instead of being on the end of your handlebars they are on the town tube of the frame. Simple stuff!

WIDE WHEEL BASE

A wide wheel base makes it safer to carry weight because it increases the stability of your bike. Look at my bike recommendations in the *Resource* section of this book, they all have a "wide" wheelbase.

BRAZE-ONS ON FRONT FORKS AND REAR FORKS

Braze-ons are a special type of threaded socket that is welded into the frame of your bicycle. They are necessary to attach most racks, and I highly recommend making sure your bike has at least four sets.

COMFORTABLE HANDLEBARS

Handle bar configuration is directly related to comfort and efficiency. Touring can be difficult, with long days on uneven roads and windy conditions. A handlebar with various hand positions will increase your overall comfort by allowing you to change your hand position often. This is the key to a good touring handlebar and is why you won't find too many flat handlebars on stock touring bikes. I only recommend two styles:

Drop Bars (personal favorite)
Drop bars allow the rider the most combinations of hand positions. I personally used a set on my touring bike, and was extremely pleased. In addition to allowing many hand positions for comfort, they allow you to optimize your aerodynamic profile for windy days or descents. When paired with bar-end shifters, you cannot find a better touring set-up. However, they do make the bike a bit harder to handle. If you are new to biking, you may prefer to use trekking bars.

Trekking Bars
Trekking bars are a favorite among many tourists, and for good reason. They allow easy access to the brakes, can be configured to have palm pads, and they allow for optimal handling of your bike. The only real downside is they limit your available hand positions.

32 SPOKES IN EACH WHEEL

The number of spokes on your wheels should not be an overlooked detail. A traditional bicycle, like a road bike, typical-

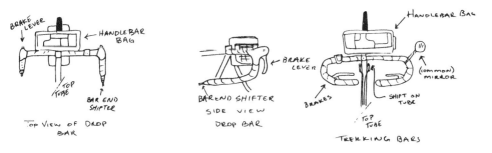

ly has about 28 or 32 spokes. This would be fine, but since you will be carrying a lot more weight than just your body, I suggest finding a bike or wheel that has at least 36 spokes. I had a Trek 520, with 36 spokes and never had one break on me. I met a few cyclists who had 28 or even 32 and had them break. This is a hit or miss event, but having more spokes will increase the strength capacity of your bike—reducing the likelihood of misfortune.

A WAY TO CARRY YOUR LOAD

By now, you may have noticed that bike touring is littered with options and flexibility! When it comes to hauling your load, you again are presented with two options:

PANNIERS

Your first option is to get a set of panniers. Personally, this is what I recommend, but it will ultimately come down to your own preference. The advantage of panniers is that you can layout your bike in an efficient manner, and still maintain a high level of maneuverability when riding. When getting a set of panniers, it is important to get a set that is waterproof.

If you decide to use panniers, you need to have a bike that comes with braze-ons (page 28), or get adapter fittings. Most bikes will come with a rack. There are two locations for panniers on your bike. The front, and rear. Most of your load will be carried in the rear of your bike, as it is the safest location both for weight and steering. I used a pair of front panniers in the beginning of my ride, and ended up mailing them home about halfway through the country because they were unnecessary for what I was traveling with.

It is important to note that the beginning of my ride was often across states with few amenities, so I hauled a lot of my food in the front bags. This is ultimately up to you, but make sure that if you get panniers, you have racks that can hold them.

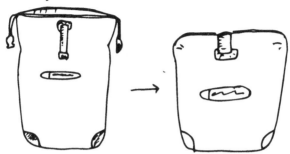

B.O.B. TRAILERS

Your second option is to get a trailer. I saw many people who used these and loved them. Basically, it is a small trailer with a dry bag enclosure for hauling all your gear. This gives you the option to haul more gear. They are still maneuverable because they are towed behind your bike. Due to this though, I would try and find one in person to check out, before you make your decision.

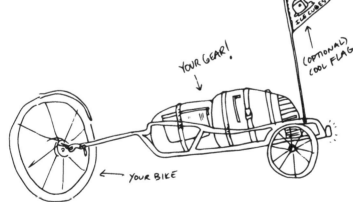

HANDLEBAR BAG

A handlebar bag is not necessary but I highly recommend it. It provides an easily accessible storage location for your camera, snacks, sunscreen, cell phone, glasses and many more useful things. You'll be happy you got one.

I bought one made by Jaand and it had a laminated map sleeve on top, which was great to have front and center while biking. You can find this bag on the marketplace at:

youcanbikeacrossamerica.com/pages/marketplace

LOADING YOUR BIKE

    Whether or not you decide to use bike panniers or a BOB trailer you're going to pack a little differently. However, some tips are universal.

    The most important thing to do is pack the things you will use the most close to the roll top of your panniers or BOB dry sack, so that you don't have to entirely unpack just to get your rain jacket or an extra layer, for example. When using panniers, pack your gear so that it is evenly distributed throughout your bicycle. This will eliminate speed wobbles during descents.

    Additionally, I suggest getting in the habit of packing all your things away in the same order and location each day. This may sound over-kill, but it actually makes locating items much easier. Since both panniers and a BOB trailer are essentially black holes that contain your gear, it is nice to add some sort of order to the chaos.

    On the Right you will find a basic illustration of where to pack items onto your bike.

GEAR

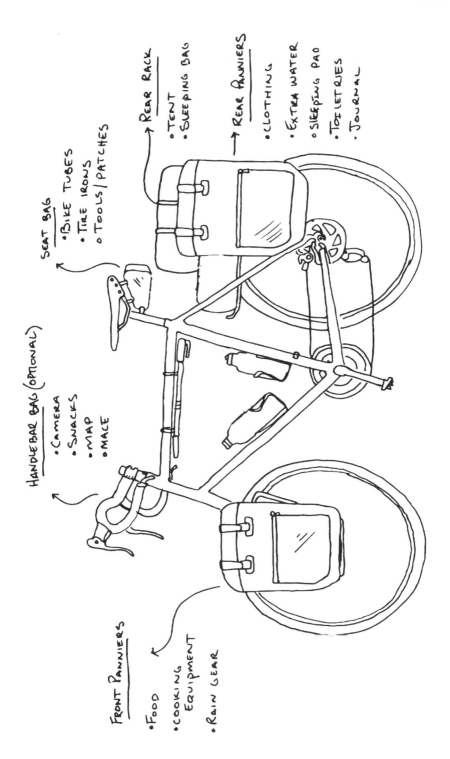

YOUR BIKE 33

RECOMMENDED UPGRADES

Chances are, your bike will not come with all these things. They are not necessary, but I think they are worth every penny to have installed—and you can do it all yourself. I have included the upgrades I performed on my bicycle, as well as put forth my recommendation for which brand or type of upgrade you should get. You will also see a price next to it, so you can decide if you'd like to do the same.

PEDALS

Install clipless pedals if your bike does not come with them already. I had a pair of Shimano 50/50 pedals that were incredible. Having your feet clipped in increases your pedal stroke efficiency by a considerable amount, especially when multiplied by the hours you will spend riding.

SHIMANO 50/50: ~$40

*Important to note that your shoes should be compatible with your clipless pedals. I used a pair of touring specific shoes from Specialized®, with a recessed clip so that I could walk without "clacking".

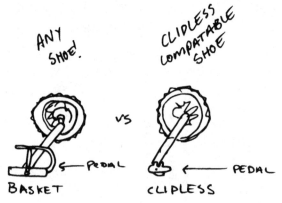

WIRELESS SPEEDOMETER

Speedometers are great because they calculate your current speed, average speed and distance traveled daily and as a complete trip. It is not necessary, but I enjoyed using mine enough to recommend it.

CAT-EYE SPEEDOMETER: ~$40

COMFORTABLE SEAT

I cannot stress enough how important a comfortable seat is. As soon as I bought my bike, the stock seat was removed and replaced. Fortunately my Great Uncle had donated a beautiful Brooks England® leather seat (B17) to me prior to my ride. It was the single most important upgrade to my bike that was made. My butt never got sore, and I could comfortably ride for eight hours a day. Had it been for a stock seat, I would be writing a different story. It became clear to me that Brooks were the best seat around when I encountered other tourists on the road. Among many, one man sticks out…

THE GREATEST SALESMAN

I had just crossed the state line into Minnesota and was riding on Route 75 just outside of Comstock, when on the horizon of the highway I could make out a black dot on the side of the road. I proceeded for a few more minutes, and when I was close enough, the other cyclist and I exchanged a few waves. The road was devoid of all traffic, and had been for the past hour. I proceeded across the double yellow line, and came to a halt on the shoulder as the man slowed to a stop in front of me. A typical meet and greet.

He was an older gentleman, with a flowing white beard and humble stature. He had been riding his bike for about a month and a half at this point, having started in Maine. However, it became very clear that this man was not new to touring. His Brooks saddle, which I admit was hardly a saddle at this point but rather a hammock, seemed to be in disrepair.

"How many miles do you have on your Brooks?" I inquired.

He chuckled while he ran his fingers along the leather, "by the time I make it to the West Coast, I will have logged over 15,000 on this one."

I could hardly believe it, as my own had just about 2,000 at this point and still looked brand-new.

"Is it comfortable?" I asked, already formulating his answer in my mind.

"It's the best damn bicycle saddle money can buy" he said, looking me square in the eyes.

So there he was, the greatest salesman for Brooks that ever lived, on the side of the road with me in the middle of Minnesota.

BROOKS B17: ~$145

BIKE LIGHT

I put a Nightrider Lumia® 750 on my bike, and then never used it because I was always done biking around 5:00pm. However, since completing my trip, I use this light daily throughout the summer and cannot say enough good things about it! I am sure that had I not bought it, Murphy's law would have had me regretting it.

NIGHTRIDER LUMIA: ~$60

BAR TAPE

This is something that can be easily overlooked until your stock tape is in tatters. A good tape is only about $12.00, but it makes a big difference in comfort. Plus, it is a great way to add some personality and class to your bike.

CORK TAPE: ~$12

EXTRA BOTTLE HOLDERS

Most bikes will come with at least one water bottle cage, but I recommend that you use at least two or even three (like I did). Water is essential to your health and to your ability to bike long distances every day, so you need to places to store it on your bike. There are many types of cages all made from different materials. I found that cheap plastic ones are best due to their weight and cost to replace if they break.

FRAME BOTTLE CAGES: ~$15 FOR 3

CAMPING

Camping equipment is relatively straightforward and can be divided into two sections; camping and cooking, as these are really the only times you'll use this gear.

CAMPING EQUIPMENT

TENT

I recommend getting a two man tent if you are going solo because it will allow extra space to put your panniers inside. This is a nice convenience.

The tent that I used was a Big Agnes Copper Spur UL 2. I cannot say enough good things about it. This tent was ideal for a solo tour for many reasons.

For one, Big Agnes has a lifetime warranty on all their products, so you can rest assured that if something happens to your tent on the road you are in good hands. Second, the Copper Spur UL 2 comes with two side entry doors, which makes entering and exiting the tent very easy, and can allow for excellent airflow when it is hot at night. Additionally, this tent fits perfect on top of a rear rack, and only weighs two pounds and twelve ounces!

SLEEPING BAG

If you are biking across the United States between May and September, a 30 to 20 degree down sleeping bag will be ideal, synthetic works just as well.

I recommend using a Big Agnes Skeeter 20. It is a 20 degree down bag, featuring Big Agnes' signature REM pad sleeve. This is a sleeve that's attached to the bottom of the bag, ensuring that you've got a solid sleeping platform and can't roll off your pad in your sleep. It really makes camping better than sleeping in your bed.

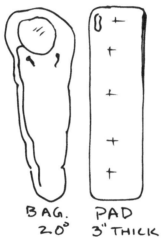

SLEEPING PAD

Do not overlook comfort, make sure that you can rest well! I recommend getting an insulated pad that is about 3" thick. I think that air filled pads are typically more comfortable than closed-cell-foam pads.

To round it out with one more incredible product, look no further than the Big Agnes Q-Core SLX. It packs smaller than a Nalgene bottle, and inflates by mouth with only a couple of breaths. You'll be sleeping like a baby, ready to tackle the day with vim and vigor.

ADDITIONAL GEAR FOR CAMP

Among the necessities, there are a few things I would highly recommend you get. These items will make life better when you settle in at camp, wherever that may be!

Headlamp
Batteries
Lighter
Toiletries
    Tooth brush
    Toothpaste
    Soap
    Floss
    Razor
Book
Journal
Knife (cooking and utility)
Seasoning kit (can be assembled from a grocery store deli)

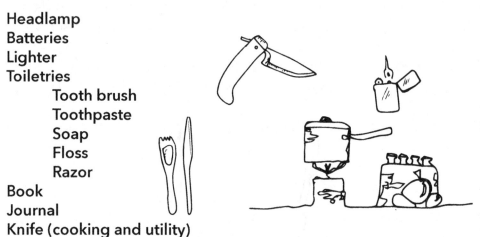

COOKING EQUIPMENT

Pack the things that you will need to cook and consume food on your bike tour. Simple!

Gas Stove w/ Extra Fuel Cartridge
JetBoil® makes excellent stoves, particularly for people who like hot beverages and one pot meals. If you prefer to cook your camp meals over a stove burner, I suggest getting a Primus® burner, or an MSR® stove that doesn't require being attached to the heat source (such as JetBoil®).

Water Filter
If you end up camping next to flowing water, having a

water filter is great because you can use that water instead of the water you already have clean for drinking. Additionally, you can fill up before you set out for tomorrow's ride! Sawyer® makes my favorite filters.

Pot or pan

Camp pots often come in compact sets of two that will store your stove burner and fuel between them. I suggest finding one of those. GSI® is a good brand to look at, as well as Sea to Summit®.

Eating Utensils

I like titanium utensils because they are light and easy to clean, but all utensils are practically the same thing. Just get what you like.

Cutting board

I used a really thin plastic one and I was thoroughly impressed with its versatility and ease of use.

Knife

I had a 3.5" Gerber® folding pocketknife, and used it multiple times everyday. It especially came in handy when making sandwiches, or cutting vegetables for dinner.

Dry Sack

I prefer to store my food in a dry sack, within my pannier. Especially high threat items, such as honey... This will mitigate disastrous spills in your panniers.

Camp Suds® and a sponge

You'll want a small thing of soap to clean your cooking equipment, utensils, hands... Do not overlook this!

TOOLS AND EXTRA

It is really important that before you head out on your bike tour you have the proper tools to deal with unexpected situations.

BIKE TOOL

A great bike tool will have a range of allen keys, a chain link tool, a metal tire iron, a bottle opener, and a screw-driver. This is absolutely essential to have! If you use fenders or braze-ons you will end up using this tool almost daily to ensure your bike is tightened correctly.

Some tools and other items in this section can be found at youcanbikeacrossamerica.com/pages/marketplace

TIRE IRONS

A plastic set will do, although I snapped every plastic one that I had by the end of my trip, so I would advise getting metal ones—just be extra cautious of your tires with them.

Over the course of my trip, I had nine flat tires. Amazingly, when my father biked across the country in 1990, he managed to get across without a single flat!

PUMP

It is crucial that you have a pump with you. I went ahead and bought myself a mini-pump, which I realized was a mistake. It was too small to get my tires to a rating of 110 PSI, so I would have to bumble along until I had a full size pump, often stopping at bike shops. What I recommend you do, is buy a full-frame pump, that mounts on your top tube. Now I will use a full-frame pump every time I go touring.

TUBES & PATCH KIT

It is necessary to carry at least two spare tubes with you at all times. The last thing you want to happen is encounter a bad flat where it cannot be patched, and you don't have extra tubes. Make sure you get the correct size for your tires.

It is worth purchasing a patch kit as well, often times your tube will have a single hole in it; once that is patched, it'll be able to be used safely until you can find the time to fully replace your tube.

TIRES

Some people carry extra tires with them, some people (myself included) do not. If I was biking somewhere totally remote, I would have an extra tire. The majority of roads in the U.S. will be fairly forgiving on your tires, and if you need to replace one, there will be a bike shop within range. However, the choice is up to you, and if you want to carry one, look into fold-able tires. You can find them on the marketplace.

SPOKES

Depending on your bike, it may come with an extra spoke on the frame that is fit for your tire. Breaking spokes, in my experience, is uncommon—but it does happen.

Something I would recommend getting is a fiber spoke. They only cost a few dollars, and if you are in a pinch, they can save the day. Most touring bikes will have 36 spokes (like my Trek 520), which is a substantial number in terms of weight bearing loads.

ROUTINE MAINTENANCE

There are a few things that you should get in the habit of doing every night before you go to sleep, or each morning when you wake up. Such things include;

Tightening all braze-ons
Tightening your racks
Checking your brakes
Checking tire pressure
Examining the condition of your tire and tread
Examining your gear's functionality

APPAREL

Look, the bottom line is that you are biking across the country. You do not need to bring a bunch of clothing. You will find that riding in the same shirt as the day before is acceptable, and your favorite pair of riding shorts will make it for the long haul—and no one is going to judge you for it. Well, some people will, but are they riding across the country? No.

SHIRTS

I am a huge fan of cycling jerseys. They are light weight, and have a great pocket configuration that makes storing snacks hassle free and accessible while riding. Others prefer a simple cotton T-shirt which I could never recommend. Truly, it is up to you.

BIKING SHORTS

Having a comfortable pair of biking shorts is imperative. You will essentially be living in them! I recommend getting shorts with a chamois (sounds like, *shammy*). This is just a pad that is formed into the shorts themselves to give you butt some more padding. Depending on your shorts, you may want to also invest in some Chamois Butt'r®. Chaffing will end your trip!

BIKING SHOES

Hopefully you have clipless pedals. The ideal biking shoe for touring will have a recessed clip so that when you walk, let's say in a grocery store, you don't clank around the whole time. Rather, it is like walking in a normal shoe.

I also recommend getting bungee laces for your shoes. I bought them on a whim, and was stoked about the purchase daily. Think about the number of times you will take your shoes on and off every day!

HELMET

I cannot stress the importance of wearing a helmet enough. It is just something you should do. You may feel confident in your ability to stay on your bike, and I understand that. However, you do not and will not have control over people driving cars on the road, or of the many animals that you will encounter.

Another great reason to wear a helmet is that you can get a mirror to attach to it so you do not have to crane your neck to see cars behind you. It is worth mentioning that the act of craning one's neck while riding in the shoulder of a road is the most dangerous thing you can possibly do! When you crane your neck, you run the risk of unintentionally steering your bike into the road in-front of traffic—as well as missing obstacles in front of you.

LAYERS

Most likely, you will be biking in the summer season. It still gets chilly in the morning, so I recommend having a pair of performance tights and a thin micro-wool top. Even a pair of light gloves. I used these more times than I could count.

Wool is an ideal material for your layers, as well as your

socks. Wool wicks moisture, and regulates temperature all while not holding odor. It is truly the best!

I also recommend that you bring a pair of comfortable pants as well as a light jacket for when you are at camp, or taking a rest day in a town or city. Biking clothes are cool, but aren't the best for relaxing at camp'.

WEATHER APPAREL

The rain may take you by surprise, so make sure that you are prepared. Ideally, your panniers are waterproof, so the only thing you need in addition to that is a fully waterproof jacket and rain pants. If you can help it, don't get rain gear that is insulated, as fully waterproof layers typically don't breathe so you will be hot.

BIKING GLOVES

You do not need to use biking gloves, but I recommend them. All the time you will spend biking will certainly take its toll on your palms, and biking gloves are the best line of defense against fatigue and cramps. That is, aside from a great bar tape (P. 37). Biking gloves come in a range of styles and materials, and as expected, they all have different pros and cons. Personally, I am a fan of traditional leather pads with a woven back for airflow (and rad sun burn patterns!).

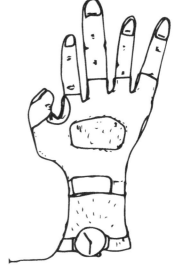

SECTION FOUR
ON RIDING

SAFETY

Simply put, safety should be your number one concern on a cross country bike ride. If you get injured your trip will be compromised, or even worse, your life will be compromised.

LOADED BIKES

The most important thing to know and understand is that when you're biking on a fully loaded bike, it is going to handle differently than a bike with no weight at all. This is especially important to understand when you're biking down a mountain pass.

On my bike trip when I was descending Washington pass, I got such bad speed wobbles from an uneven distribution of weight on my bike that I had to pinch the frame with my knees* as hard as I possibly could until the bottom. It was terrifying, but it taught me the importance of evenly packing a touring bike. From that point on, I had no issues.

What I did not do, and what I recommend that you do is, fully load up your bike prior to your tour and go see what it's like to go fast on l loaded bike. Seems like a no-brainer, right?

SHOULDERS

If you're not used to biking in the shoulder of the road I highly recommend that you start practicing. It may not seem like a big deal, but once you're in the middle of a pass climbing up in the shoulder and cars are flying by at 50+ miles an hour, or a logging truck or RV is approaching from behind, it's a big deal and the last thing you need is to feel uncomfortable and wobble into the road.

My dad told me prior to my ride, "Own the road". What he meant by that was to take my portion out of the shoulder of the road so that I had room for error. This cannot be overstressed. See the illustration below.

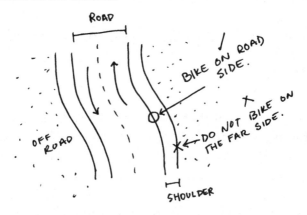

TIRE PRESSURE

Every bike and tire manufacturer is going to have a different specification for tire pressure. Make sure that you check your recommended PSI and adjust accordingly.

REFLECTORS

Visibility is the difference between getting hit by a truck, and staying on your bicycle in one piece. You may not be able to control how drivers react, but you can control how visible you are to them. Regardless of the time of day, you should have at least a red blinking reflector on your bike, and rear reflectors. My favorite panniers, made by Ortleib®, come standard with rear reflectors on them!

If you are ever going to be biking around dusk, get a bike light. (P. 36)

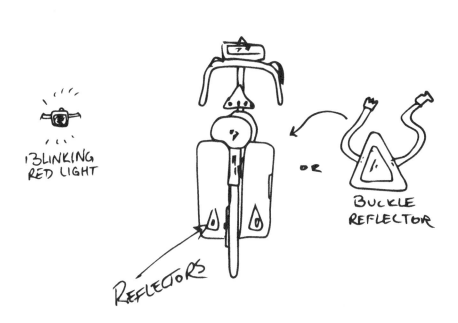

EFFICIENCY

BEST TIME TO RIDE

I found the best time to ride is early in the morning, while the sun is still coming up. Early in the day the temperature is often the coolest it will be which makes for great riding. It is also quiet, as the world is waking up. It is very enjoyable! I found that starting early was the key to being able to crank out a good mileage total for the day.

I would always try my best to finish more than half of my miles by lunch. Psychologically, it made the rest of the day easier. Also, starting early eliminates having to bike into the night, or falling short on mileage due to unknown circumstances. Plus, who doesn't love an alpine start?

THIS WAS A TYPICAL BIKE-TOUR DAY FOR ME:

6:30am - Wake up, make breakfast
7:30am -Break down camp
8:00am - On the road biking
1:00pm - Break for lunch
      I would try and have more than half my day's miles done by lunch, this is a physiological trick. Now there is less to do

for the second half of the day—when it is hot and you're getting tired.
1:30/2:00pm - Back on the road
5/6:00pm - Be at camp destination
7:00pm - Eat dinner and check state map, locate an end of day location for tomorrow
8:00pm - Read and write in my tent
9:00pm - Asleep!

You will notice that in a day, I spend about 8 hours biking. That was typical. Sometimes more, sometimes less. You will find your rhythm. When I was picking an end of day location, I would shoot for 80-100 miles out from where I was camping. This is why a state map came in handy, since it gave me superior flexibility. Also, it gave town size, so I could judge the availability of a camping location. With the aid of the Internet, I was able to Google for campgrounds, satellite view for public parks, dugouts, etc. or even call city halls and ask about where it would be alright for me to camp free of charge.

It is important to note that biking is largely about pace. The task is to find a pace that works for you, and then maximize the amount of time going that pace. Biking across the country seems daunting at first, but broken down into manageable segments of 80 to 100 mile days makes it all seem a lot more plausible. That being said, this is your bike tour—not someone else's—so go the mileage that you find works for you.

CADENCE

Cadence is the fancy word for pedal crank rotations per minute. This is an important thing to keep track of because it not only relates to efficiency, it also can prevent injury.

It is my recommendation that you should always try and have a cadence between 80 and 120. This can be optimized by your gearing.

I was biking across Washington State with a father and his 24-year-old daughter that I had met. As we were finishing a climb up a pass she started to notice aching pain in her knee, so I asked her about her cadence. She replied to me that she wasn't paying attention to her cadence but she preferred to push harder gears, rather than spin a lighter gear. I suggested she try switching to a higher (easier) gear, despite her preferences. Lo and behold by the end of that day, her knee began to feel better! It puts less strain on your body to spin faster and push lighter.

When you are riding a long flat day, finding a cadence in the range of 80 and 120 is ideal because it requires that you bike at a moderate pace without too much muscular strain. If you push a harder gear, you may go faster, but it will take more effort.

A simple way to find you cadence while biking is to count how many times your right foot hits the bottom of its stroke over 15 seconds, and then multiply that by four.

WIND

If you have a tail-wind, use it! Wind will dramatically increase your ability to knock off high mileage days, granted it's a tailwind. If, on the other hand, it's a headwind you're in for a long day.

TERRAIN

Increasing your efficiency on a day-to-day basis will have a lot to do with the terrain that you're experiencing. For example, if you're riding a long flat day just find a cadence and a rhythm that works for you and maximize your hours spent biking. If you're biking up a mountain pass, understand that the pass is going to be the slowest portion of the day, but once you get to the top you'll make up your average miles an hour on the way down. Plan accordingly!

REST DAYS

Rest days are crucial if you want to be able to bike free of injury and mental distress. At least in my own experience I find this true.

On June 21st I was biking into Republic, Washington, after summiting Wauconda pass—a brutal 27 mile climb situated at the end of a 40 mile day ride—that left me exhausted and dehydrated.

During the final portion of the descent I heard a loud explosion under my rear rack, and began to lose control of my bicycle at 38 miles an hour. Miraculously, I was able to tame my machine and slow to a halt in a pull-out. Upon inspection, it was clear that I had punctured my tire and popped my tube. Evening was rushing in and I was still 16.5 miles out of Republic—ah, the tribulations of adventure. I unloaded my panniers and flipped my bike upside down to begin replacing the tube, and patching my tire. That is until I was shafted by my own unpreparedness. I had no spare tubes in my pannier.

I swallowed my pride and started trying to thumb my way into town. After about 15 minutes, a pickup truck pulled over and a gentleman rolled down the passenger window to speak with me. Delighted to help a young cross-country cyclist, he helped load up my gear and brought me right to the police station—upon my request. I was at my wits end. I had been biking for a week straight at this point, eight hours a day, climbing a total of seven mountain passes.

In the station, I asked the receptionist if there was anywhere I could camp for free in town. I was told that the closest place with free camping was 15 miles out of town at the fair grounds. Not only did I not have the daylight to get there, I didn't have a bike that rolled! It was then that I made arguably the best decision of my trip—I called my mom. Through exhausted tears, I proclaimed that I was quitting my bike trip. Delusional? Absolutely. "Isaiah, can I just put you up in a motel for the night? You can rest and deal with your bike tomorrow. I know you are strong enough to complete this trip, you're just tired," my mom insisted.

Relieved and dumbfounded, I walked my bike to the nearest motel. The thought of taking a rest day hadn't occurred to me as a possibility until just then, and man did it sound incredible. The next morning, I woke up at 10 am, went about my errands to get tubes and food at the grocery store in town. I am not a TV watcher, but when I went back to my motel room all I did was lay down on my bed and watch TV the whole day, and for the first and only time in my life, I loved it. The next day I woke up refreshed and clear headed, ready to continue tackling the United States by bike. By chance, two other cyclists happened to be staying at the motel I ended up at and had an extra tube. Rock on!

CENTENNIAL RIDES

Centennial rides are an excellent thing to put in your quiver for knocking off mileage. The trick to completing a centennial ride (100 miles or more), in my opinion, is being able to knock out more than half of the miles before lunch.

Technology can be your ally. A feature that I used was Google Maps. On Google Maps you can look at your daily route and actually see real-time elevation, which you can then use to determine how fast you can go throughout mileage points. I used this a lot to know what I was in for before I actually started riding (page 19).

MOST IMPORTANT FACTOR

The single most important factor to biking efficiently and having a successful tour is your ability to have fun and enjoy the opportunity that you have to bike across the United States. If you are not having a good time, everything is going to feel difficult.

ON RIDING

Your attitude determines your aptitude, and with bike touring that is especially true!

EFFICIENCY 57

CLIMBING PASSES

WILL YOU HAVE TO CLIMB PASSES?

Chances are that if you are biking across the United States you're going to have to climb a pass or two. It will ultimately depend on the route that you decide to ride. On my specific route I climbed eight mountain passes in six days, then didn't climb one for over a month and a half! (This is why I started on the West Coast!)

THE CLIMB

Prior to my bike tour, I was a little intimidated of biking up mountain passes. After all, I had never biked up one. However, after my first ascent I realized that climbing a mountain pass is in fact one of the greatest feelings that once can experience on a bike, second only to careening down the other side at full speed (I can be a speed freak...)

There are times when the climb alone will take five hours. Since it can take so long, I recommend having some source of entertainment or a mindfulness meditation practice to accompany your pedaling. On the first day, I tried listening to music. After the first album played through I realized music simply wasn't going to

ON RIDING

cut it. Personally, the music just got boring. So, I ended up turning to audio books and podcasts.

Audio books and podcasts changed the game for me. I could now bike for a whole entire day and crank through a whole entire book. I love reading, but on my bike tour by the time I got to my tent I was often too tired to pick up a book. Audio books were the next best thing.

MY RECOMMENDED PODCASTS

RADIOLAB

INVISIBILIA

SNAP JUDGEMENT

THE TIM FERRISS PODCAST

HARDCORE HISTORY

THIS AMERICAN LIFE

SERIAL

TIPS FOR MAKING THE CLIMB EASIER

Perhaps the most difficult part of a climb is the psychological aspect. I found it extremely helpful to simply focus on the task at hand which is pedaling. What I mean by this is that you shouldn't focus on how far you have to go to get to the top, but rather focus on what you have to do in this moment to continue progress.

If the pass is so steep you feel like you just can't make any progress, try zigzagging across your lane. This zigzagging motion

CLIMBING PASSES 59

reduces the amount of effort you have to expend to make forward progress by reducing the path's gravitational force on you. This can be a safety concern, however. So it is important to make sure that you are absolutely certain the lane is clear for you to begin riding in a zig-zag fashion. Then there is always the...

GEARS

Use easy gears when climbing passes, and have the mechanics of the bicycle do the work. If you have to stand up on your bike to make progress, chances are you are doing too much work, and should down-shift. Climbing up should be done in low, high spinning gears. When descending, you should shift to higher gears that require more effort. This ensures a proper cadence that is safe and efficient. When in doubt, spin it out!

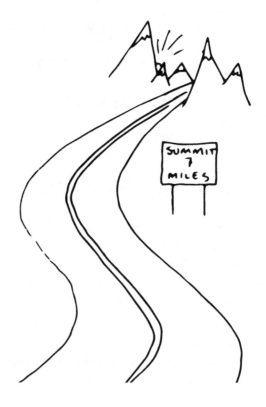

TOWNS

PICKING TOWNS TO BIKE THROUGH

Since I was creating my route on a day-to-day basis, it was important to pick specific towns I knew I would bike through. The resource I used most for determining if a town was worth biking through, was Google Maps.

Simply look at your State Map, determine what towns are on your specific route, then Google them on your mobile phone to see what you will be working with.

POST OFFICES

I used post offices for many things; from mailing extra items home, mailing postcards, or receiving packages that were sent to me. The cool thing about post offices are that you can send things via "general delivery" and the post office will typically hold that package for a week.

When you get into that town, you enter the post office, and show them your ID, then they give you your package. It is that simple. This can be extremely helpful if you need an extra part, or piece of equipment mailed to you along the way. Just make sure to account for shipping vs biking time so you don't end up having to be in a town for three extra days waiting!

BIKE SHOPS

The shops are always a great resource for spare parts, bike route suggestions, killing time and sharing stories. Many shops will love to talk with you about your tour, so be sure to stop in!

One of my favorite things to do on my bike tour was visit local bike shops. I'd make sure to always get a sticker from the local shop and put it on my bike. By the end of my ride I had collected over 15 unique stickers on my bike frame, all from a specific location I had been to.

GROCERY STORES

It is important to include towns that will have grocery stores on your route. This is easy towards the coasts, but in states like Montana and North Dakota, you will most likely encounter towns without grocery options. This isn't an inconvenience in a car, but when you are only using a bike it could mean 40 more miles until you can get lunch!

Among other food options, keep your eye out for local farm stands.

HOSTELS

AFFORDABLE AND RELIABLE

Although lacking in size compared to Europe, the United States has a fairly large network of hostels available for travelers. Many hostels will range in price from $15 to $35 a night. This is a great price for the hot shower, bed, electricity and community that is often present during a stay.

Throughout my trip, I was always searching for Hostels to

stay at, and although I passed up on quite a few, I was able to spend the night at a couple of great ones.

The Internet is the best resource available for finding hostels during your bike trip. Here are some hostels that I stayed at:

Winthrop, WA - North Cascade's Hostel

Conveniently located along the Route 20 Highway in Washington, you are likely to end up here if you are crossing in the Northern portion of the state. I highly recommend this hostel and town in general. It is a really interesting place, and is a time-warp back to the Wild West!

Colville, WA - Bacon Bike Hostel

Owned and operated by Shelley and Barry Bacon, this is a can't miss destination. The hostel operates on an honor system, and is on the Adventure Cycling Association's Northern Tier Route--so you will most likely encounter other cyclists here.

East Glacier - The Backpacker's Inn

If you end up staying the night in East Glacier, this is a fun and convenient hostel to stay in. It is situated in the back yard of a Mexican restaurant, which is a biker's dream, right? The Amtrak comes right through the village, so you may encounter other travelers in this small hostel.

Gackle, ND - The Honey Hostel

When I stayed here, it was free to cyclists, and had a donation box. Complete with laundry, a bunk room, showers and a massive wall of Honey Stinger products to refuel, the Honey Hostel will not disappoint.

EATING AND HYDRATION

HYDRATION

I cannot stress how critical hydration is to being able to ride across the country. You need to be drinking water all day, every day that you ride as well as on days you take off.

FILTRATION

I explained more about this on page 40. Simply put, get a water filter that you can rely on to provide safe water throughout your trip. More often than not, you'll have access to potable water, but just in case you should have a filter as well. I recommend the Sawyer® Squeeze filter, with two additional 32 oz. bladders.

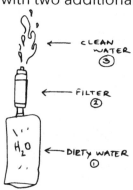

CAMEL UP

If you have not heard this phrase before, you need to hear it now. "Camel up" means drinking all the water that you currently have, in order to refill all your reservoirs at your current fill-station.

For example, say you have three bottles of water on your bike and two of them are empty from the day of riding. It is around noon, and you roll into Silo, Montana. When you get to the only building in town other than the grain silo, you realize you can fill up your water bottles. You now have the option to do two things. Fill up two bottles, and continue on, or drink the remaining water in the full bottle, then fill up all three. Trust me, it is in your best interest to camel up, and fill up all three.

Remember the water filter I was talking about earlier? Make sure you bring one because then no matter what, as long as there is water flowing, you are safe to drink it.

WHERE TO GET FOOD

Most of the time I bought my food in grocery stores. However, it is important to note that not every town is going to have a grocery store that you're used to. As in, sometimes they are quite limited in terms of what they have available to buy. There were many times where meals I had planned on being able to prepare became wishful ideas without the proper ingredients available. Keep in mind that not every town you bike through is going to have a place to eat that you are interested in.

So, what I recommend is that you look on Google Maps or your state map at the town size of the next place will be biking through. That way you can ensure that if you're in a great grocery store and the next town isn't going to be as good, you can get everything you need for the next few days of biking.

Some of my favorite things to bulk up on are trail mix, rice, beans and other things it won't go bad sitting in your panniers.

Also, get fresh fruit when you can and Apple goes along way with some peanut butter!

Finding and cooking your own food is obviously going to be much more cost-effective than trying to find a place to eat every day for every meal.

MEALS

Before my bike trip, I thought it would be a good idea to eat a big breakfast every morning so I would have the energy to get through the day. But once I started biking, I found that having a small breakfast and a big dinner was more effective for me, because a heavy breakfast left me feeling bogged down. This will vary person to person, so find what is right for you.

The reason that a handlebar bag is recommended is because you can use it to store necessities that you use every day. I found it's an extremely useful place to put snacks so you can eat on the go without having to stop your bike.

SOME OF MY FAVORITE FOODS FOR TOURING

Lentils
Quinoa
Sandwiches
Peanut butter and bananas
Avocados

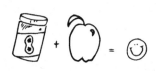

These will ripen well in your panniers quite nicely, so I would not recommend buying ripe ones unless you plan to eat them immediately.
Chocolate covered pretzels
Trail Mix
Dates
Honey Stinger® Waffles and Chews (Try them, you'll love em!)
Apples and Cheese

ON SLEEPING

THE MOST COMMON QUESTION

"Isaiah, while you were biking across the country, where did you sleep every night?"

I can't tell you how many times I've been asked this question about a bike tour. The truth is, I slept in many different places throughout my 48 day ride across United States and so will you. Unless you plan on staying in a hotel every single night you're going to have to be flexible.

From sleeping under a picnic table in a park, to dugouts on a baseball field and even stranger's houses or National Parks[1], you'll do it all. That's the beauty of bike touring; you never know what to expect!

It's really not as hard as one might think to find a place to sleep every night. However, the hard part is finding an acceptable and safe place to sleep every night. Fortunately there are many resources available to the bike tourist to aid in finding a spot.

---

1   Did you know that our National Parks and public lands are in danger? Please see Page 89 for more information on the crisis, and what you can do as an individual to help.

FINDING A PLACE TO SLEEP

I used a variety of resources for finding places to sleep and pitch my tent. Here are my go-to places (on next page):

WARM SHOWERS *(WARMSHOWERS.ORG)*

This is a website, or a smart phone app, that lays out a Google Map with specific pins where hosts sign up to house cyclists. That's right, a website platform built specifically for people on bike tours! Visit warmshowers.org to find more information about their service.

GOOGLE MAPS

Google maps is an excellent resource. Whenever I would buy can do a town I would usually pull up a satellite image of the area on Google Maps. What I would look for were green shaded areas which were more often than not, free public land. If it wasn't too far out of town, I would bike over and assess the area, and if it looked safe, I would pitch a tent out of sight.

POLICE DEPARTMENT

I cannot stress the importance of calling local Police Departments and asking for their assistance. Many of the towns that you will bike through have probably not seen many people crossing the country on a bicycle so they'll be more than happy to help! I would often call the local police department of a town and ask if they knew of any places I could pitch a tent for free. Most of the time they were extremely helpful and even offered to send a patrol car throughout the night to make sure that I was doing well and no one was bothering me.

CITY OR TOWN HALLS

Calling the city or town hall is basically the same as calling the police department in that you ask where you can pitch a tent for free, and make sure to tell them what you're doing! Again, they will most likely be extremely helpful and excited.

I was biking with a couple on their honeymoon when we rolled into a Hebron, North Dakota where we were going to stay the night. We didn't have a place to stay yet so we went in the local grocery store to get some things for dinner and ended up asking the cashier if they knew of any places that we could stay. Being a small town, the cashier told us to wait just a moment while she called her friend. Her friend was the town mayor. After no more than two minutes she was directing us to the nearest park, where the Mayor was going to meet us. Shortly after we arrived at the park a small group of people arrived. It was the Mayor and his family, along with a few friends and their children. They had all heard the news of the cross country cyclists, and wanted to visit and hear our stories and examine our bikes and gear. This is the America that I have learned to love.

When we met them they asked if there was anything that we needed that they could help with. One member of the town showed up with two cases of Gatorade—way more than we could drink or carry! I think the important thing to understand is that most people have not encountered someone biking across the United States, so when they do they want to know everything about your trip and they want to help in anyway that they can.

LOCALS

Let's admit it, it's hard to not want to know about a cyclist that's riding a fully loaded bike. So use that to your advantage. When you bike into town and you're looking for a place to say just ask the locals! Many times I would talk to a local and they would be more than happy to help in anyway that they could by offering me a place to stay, a warm shower, dinner, and often a breakfast with coffee. America, despite what the critics say, you are a country full of beautiful and generous people.

FRIENDS OR FAMILY

Use family and friends and their connections to find out if anyone you know knows someone in the town that you're in. Simple, really.

FACEBOOK

Same as above. Use the Internet. I had a Facebook page, "Follow Me Across America", and I would post updates throughout my trip, and many times someone would tell me, "Hey, I know so-and-so that lives in the next town you will be biking through, get in touch with them, they'd love to put you up!"

By the time I made it to the East Coast I was staying in a comfortable bed every night, spoiled to my hearts content.

WHAT HAPPENS WHEN YOU GET CAUGHT

I was biking late with one of my friends that I had met in Minnesota, and as a last resort we ended up at a park downtown. We set up under a pavilion, putting our sleeping pads on the concrete and going to bed under the lights of the park. I awoke from my slumber with a bright LED flashlight shining in my face. Having absolutely no idea where I was, nor what time it was I frantically began looking around as the officer said, "gentlemen can you tell me what you're doing here?"

I sat up in my sleeping bag and proclaimed, "We are biking across the United States and we got into town late last night and this is the only place we had to sleep". The officer reached for his shoulder and repeated what I had said into his radio.

The police ended up letting us stay there under the circumstance that if the neighbors around the park began to complain that we were being loud or obnoxious they would have evict us from our location. We thought this was funny because we were sleeping, prior to them waking us up.

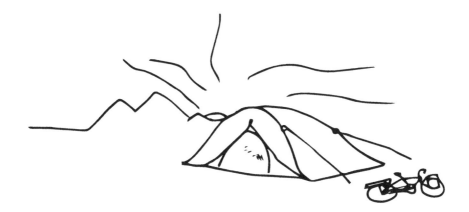

REPAIRS

As much as you would like to be in control, sometimes you simply are not. What are you to do in the event of a broken part, or another type of emergency? A huge portion of what makes bike touring such an exhilarating activity is your constant shuffle between control and the unknown. You never know if your tire is going to pop on you, or if your rack braze-ons are going to sheer. So, the bike tourist must be ready to think fast, and problem solve efficiently whenever possible. Ideally, nothing goes wrong during your bike ride—but life is everything but ideal.

My favorite resource for bike-repairs and maintenance is of course, YouTube. However, in the following pages, I have laid out a few tips for the most common problems you will encounter. Most things can be dealt with on the road, but often times if you encounter a serious issue, you'll need to see a bike shop.

TIRES

During my tour, I had nine flat tires and had to replace my chain in Wisconsin. That's about as hopeless as I ever was. I think back and am thankful for all the blown tires, because it made me quick as lightning. My first flat took me an hour to replace, and by the ninth, it took a mere three minutes.

Replacing a flat tire is the most important thing that you should know how to do if you are self-supporting across the country.

HOW TO REPLACE A FLAT TIRE

Never let a new tube touch the ground. Keep it as clean as possible, as any small debris that goes between the tube and tire will most likely cause another flat.

In the event of a flat tire, this is what you should do.

1. Down shift as much as you can then unload your bags from the bike and position it upside down.
2. Move dérailleur and unlock your brakes, then unscrew the air valve on your tube.
3. Deflate as much air from the tube as you can then insert a tire iron between the rim and tire bead.
4. Slide the iron 360 degrees around the rim, pulling off the tire. Remove the tube next.
   At this point, try and identify the hole in the tube, in relation to the tire. Inspect the tire for any debris that caused the flat. If you find anything, remove it! Use this time to clean the inside of the tire.
5. Inflate a new tube to about 20%.
6. Carefully and cleanly insert the partially inflated tube into the wheel rim, between the tire. Fit the valve through the rim hole.
7. Encase the tube completely with the tire, and put half the bead inside the rim.
8. Using the iron, maneuver the other bead onto the rim and then begin inflating.

Confused? Just give a quick search on YouTube and you'll be fixing flats in no time!

BROKEN CHAIN

Some people will say that carrying an extra chain is necessary, but I disagree. Look, if you are going to bike across the Sahara, you better carry one. Fortunately, the US is littered with bike shops, and with the Internet, it just isn't necessary to put one in your pannier. Like I mentioned above, I had to replace a chain in Wisconsin. The chain itself was intact, but it was stretched.

I noticed because I was biking out of the Mississippi River Valley and my gear kept slipping. I was about two days out from a bike shop, and it wasn't a dire situation, so I was able to make it there using limited gearing. However, it is up to you to pack one if you feel you'll need it.

SPOKES

A lot of touring bikes will come with an extra spoke; check yours. If you don't have one stock, I would get one and stash it on your bike (tape it to the frame or something), they even make fiber spokes that hardly weigh anything!

The Trek 520 is a beast of a bike because it comes standard with 36 spokes, which really translates to superior dependability compared to a traditional bike that is outfitted with 28 or 32.

For a typical cross country ride, you probably won't have enough weight to be popping spokes off, so one extra should do the trick.

SECTION **FIVE**
RESOURCES & F.A.Q.

RESOURCES

ADVENTURE CYCLING ASSOCIATION

An absolute leader in cycling maps, ACA has complete map kits for cross country rides available on their website. Even if you decide not to buy their maps (like I did), they have a lot of useful information for free available. I highly advise becoming a member of ACA, and subscribing to their Adventure Cyclist magazine. It will certainly curb your itch to get on the road!

Their map kits typically cost around $150, and include 5-12 sections of maps. I essentially did their Northern Tier Route, but had the flexibility to go "off-route" when I wanted to, using my state maps.

STATE MAPS

State maps can frequently be found in gas stations and are around $11. There are a few brands I would recommend, just based on my experience of relevant information and paper size. Rand McNally makes my favorite maps, they are the ideal size for day rides and fit in most map sleeves on handlebar bags.

RAILS TO TRAILS

Traillink.com is a website you should explore. Rails to Trails is an organization that focuses on trails that have been converted from old train track routes. So they remove the tracks, and usually lay down some form of rock--many trails featured a smooth limestone mix that was great for biking.

Every day I would look at my route, and then cross reference to see if any RTC trails were available. They are beautiful trails and often take you along a way you would otherwise never travel.

From their website's "About Us" page:

Rails to Trails Conservancy (RTC) serves as the national voice for more than 160,000 members and supporters, 31,000 miles of rail-trails and multi-use trails, and more than 8,000 miles of potential trails waiting to be built, with a goal of creating more walkable, bike-able communities in America.

DAVID KEIFER ARTICLE

http://www.upi.com/Archives/1987/09/18/A-one-legged-bicyclist-seeking-to-regain-the-cross-country-handi-capped/9817558936000/

THE SUN STANDS NO CHANCE.

GEAR COST LIST

SPECIFIC RECOMMENDATIONS CAN BE FOUND ON
youcanbikeacrossamerica.com/pages/marketplace

Prices are subject to change, and do not necessarily reflect the exact cost of your tour. This is what you may expect to spend. Remember, you may have a lot of these things already!

$1500	Bike	$5	Soap
$50	50/50 Pedals	$5	Floss
$180	Brooks Seat (B17)	$10	Razor
$30	Water Bottles (3)	$5	Shaving Cream
$60	Handlebar Bag	$450	Tent
$120	Rear Pannier Set (2)	$150	Sleeping Bag
$100	Front Pannier Set (2)	$100	Pad
$60	Front Rack	$40	Biking Shorts
$70	Back Rack	$40	Jersey
$45	Fender Set	$70	Wool base-layers
$40	Speedometer	$45	Helmet
$65	Bike Light (Bright LED)	$15	Helmet Mirrored
$20	Blinking Red Light	$10	Journal
$60	Bike Pump (Full Size)	N/A	Camera
$30	Bike Tool	N/A	GoPro or similar
$20	Tire Irons	$60	SD Card(s)
$15	Chain Lube	$20	Headphones
$10	Extra braze-on screws (5x)	$10	Matches
$50	Spare Tire	$4	Lighter
$40	Tubes (x3)	$45	Headlamp
$40	Camp Stove	$35	Bike Gloves
$12	Gas for stove	$40	Water Filter
$15	Bear Spray	$15	Dry Bag
$10	Utensils	$30	Pocketknife
$5	Toilet Paper (2x)		
$5	Toothbrush	**Total:**	$3,856.00

RECOMMENDED BIKES

These prices reflect the research I have done at the time of writing this book, so naturally they are subject to change. I like these bikes because they are truly high quality and will be a bike you have long after your cross-country bike tour. I still ride my Trek 520 all the time!

All bikes come in a range of frame sizes. To get the best fit, please visit your local bike shop, as they will be more than happy to outfit you properly. Bikers love helping bikers!

CO-MOTION® CASCADIA - $1945.00

TREK® 520 - $1359.99

SURLY® LONG HAUL TRUCKER - $1274.00

REI® CO-OP ADV. 1 - $1099.00

JAMIS® AURORA - $929.00

Craigslist and your local bike shop are also great places to look for other bikes!

FREQUENTLY ASKED QUESTIONS

In this section of the book, I have organized and answered many of the most common questions that I have been asked, and still get asked about my bike tour across the United States.

F.A.Q.

I WANT TO GET SPONSORED FOR MY RIDE, HOW DO I DO IT?

I was able to get sponsored by many local businesses in my hometown, as well as a few bigger companies. I cannot guarantee that you will be able to get sponsored, but if you want to give it a try, this is what I did and what I recommend.

First and foremost, commit to your ride. No one will accept your sponsorship if they feel like you will back out. It is also important to have a system of accountability set up. What I mean by this is to have some sort of online presence, whether it is Instagram, a Facebook page, or a blog. I had all three, and through those platforms I was able to help promote my sponsors in exchange for their support.

Another important factor in getting sponsored is being

able to ask effectively. Simply requesting sponsorship for your bike ride across the country will not do it. Rather, if you are approaching a local business for financial support, make sure that you can tell them exactly how their funds will benefit your trip–then be sure to use them exactly for what you said.

It goes without saying that if a business agrees to sponsor you in any way, you should follow up with a thank you letter of some form. Also, do not be afraid to e-mail bigger companies and ask for their sponsorship policies!

Granted you get individuals or businesses to agree, you can now get creative in how you promote them through your platforms. I had a page on my website that listed my sponsors, and would post on my Facebook page about them and their support which made my ride possible. I also had made T-shirts to raise my own funds, and included sponsors on the back of the shirt. Get creative!

HOW DID YOU ALIGN YOURSELF WITH A NON-PROFIT?

In a similar way to finding a sponsor, seek a non-profit that you feel passionately about and reach out to tell them what you are doing. E-mail is often the best way to reach them initially. Most non-profits have systems in place and people that can assist you with aligning.

Throughout my ride I collected donations both in person, as well as through my website for an organization called the USANA True Health Foundation. I had personally met the President of the foundation, and discussed how we could work together.

A bike tour is a great platform for supporting a non-profit because not only does it add value to your already personal journey, but it also allows for great exposure to your cause because of the distance you will travel and the audience you can develop.

WERE YOU WORRIED ABOUT STRANGERS? MEAN PEOPLE?

Personally, not at all. I was excited about being able to truly meet the people of the United States! Prior to my ride, I had many people tell me that I should be worried about people who would potentially steal my bike or other equipment—suggesting I stay on my toes. I found this way of thinking to be ridiculous. I am a firm believer that one attracts what one thinks about. So instead of worrying, I was thankful for the opportunity to ride my bike and meet nice, friendly and interested people. In the end, I never encountered anyone who wanted to do me harm in any way. Despite what people may say, the people who live and work in this country and warm and welcoming and more than happy to help a traveler.

WHAT WAS THE ONE TOOL YOU COULD NOT LIVE WITHOUT?

My bike multi-tool. It had an allen set, which I used often, as well as a metal tire iron and chain-link remover. It was compact, and versatile.

I also would be doing a disservice if I did not mention the usefulness of a smartphone. From emergency calls and directions, to quick camera shots and audio-entertainment, a smartphone was priceless.

HOW DID YOU PLAN BIKING WITH REGARD TO WEATHER?

I simply planned on biking every day regardless of the weather because I knew I had the gear and clothing to handle whatever nature threw at me. I only got into trouble with weather once, and it was due to my own faulty decision making. In Wisconsin, I had mailed home a lot of extra items that I wasn't using.

Among them was my rain-pants. Having not encountered rain in over 2,500 miles, I decided to shave some weight and mail them home. Fast forward about a week and a half, I am biking across Pennsylvania, and I had to stop and do laps in a grocery store pushing an empty cart (to look like I was shopping) for over an hour to warm up because the rain had been so heavy all day. That was as intense as the weather got! Learn from my mistake, and do not mail home rain gear!

WHY DID YOU DECIDE TO MAKE THIS TRIP? HOW DID IT MEASURE UP TO WHAT YOU EXPECTED? WHERE DID IT FAIL?

I decided to do this trip because it simply got me excited in a way that nothing in my life had up until that point. It was a true adventure, and something I knew I would be able to recall for the rest of my life—as I still do. I wanted to grow as an individual and experience something that was genuinely difficult—something that would test my mind and body like never before.

Simply put, it blew my expectations clean off the map. The day after I finished my trip I slept in for the first time in over two months, and I remember having thought to myself, "I am going to be unpacking that trip for a long time". There was just simply too much that I had experienced to grasp the magnitude in a few days of recovery. Still to this day I make new connections or associations to the trip unlocking new memories. I grow everyday because of it.

It didn't fail me at all.

WOULD YOU DO IT AGAIN? IF SO, WHAT WOULD YOU CHANGE?

Absolutely, I *will* do it again. In regards to what I would change, it is simple; I would pack less. I had packed a lot of clothing that I never wore once. Clothes don't weigh much, but they do take up space that is valuable in panniers. I would also bike all the way up to the coast of Maine, maybe even into Nova Scotia. I have spent some time in Maine, and it is an incredibly beautiful state and I would imagine it is a biker's dream.

WHAT WAS SOMETHING YOU THOUGHT WOULD BE IMPORTANT WHEN YOU FIRST STARTED PLANNING THAT TURNED OUT NOT TO BE?

I thought it would be important to know exactly where I would stop every night prior to even beginning my ride. After the first few days, I took a more laid back approach and planned only one day ahead, as I was going to bed in my tent. The beauty of a trip such as this, is that you have complete flexibility—so there is no need to over-plan.

WHERE YOU AFRAID OF LONELINESS BEFORE THE TRIP STARTED?

Yes, but in a strange way. I was more unsure of how I would handle it than being afraid of it. I embraced the opportunity to be on my own for the first time in my life for an extended period of time. By nature, I enjoy solitude—so it felt natural once I settled into the groove of everyday riding. However, I never felt truly alone because I met so many people on the road—and I am a social person who loves to talk with locals and tell stories of my own.

HOW MUCH DO YOU NEED TO WORK OUT BEFORE THE RIDE ITSELF?

I am being brutally honest here; anyone can do this trip. I truly believe that. For the sake of answering this with some substance though, let me say this:

I was 18 years old, and was a Varsity Cross Country runner, so I was in great shape, physically. However, this only aided me in the physical portion of the ride. Most of the ride's difficulty is fought in the mental arena. You need to be able to persevere mentally more often than physically. Riding up a mountain pass is going to test your ability to focus rather than your legs ability to push another pedal stroke.

HOW DID YOU FIND PLACES TO SHOWER? POOP?

Simply put, by biking past them. Maybe it was just me or maybe it was sitting on a bike seat all day, but I conveniently never had to poop while riding my bike in the middle of nowhere. Rather, I only had to when I was in the presence of a gas station, town or campground. Finding a place to pee is rookie business.

Showers usually took place at campgrounds, and when someone would let me stay at their house I amply took advantage of their shower—every time. I am still thankful for all of their generosity.

WHAT DOES YOUR EMERGENCY REPAIR KIT LOOK LIKE?

I had a minimalistic attitude towards mechanical problems. Maybe it was naive, but it didn't land me in trouble. My repair kit contained:
Two spare tubes (always)
Bike Tool (P.65)
Tube Patch Kit
TearAid®
Spoke

There was a time in Michigan that I "patched" a tube by fitting a candy bar wrapper between my tube and tire. It was enough to get me to the next town, where I ultimately had to replace my rear tire at a bike shop. My point is, your repair kit might not always be the thing saving the day.

WHERE WAS YOUR FAVORITE PLACE TO BIKE THROUGH?

Glacier National Park blew my mind and stole my heart. It epitomized the trip in its entirety, if that is at all possible. It entertained endless natural beauty, while at the same time reminding me of this country's dark past. Being the last portion of mountains moving East before you enter Browning, it provides a stark contrast between Native American reservations, and their original land. In the park there is lush forest, open lakes and steep mountain faces colliding with crisp air. Nature, although surrounded by developments within the park, is alive and dominant.

Still to this day, it has left the greatest impact on me from my bicycle travels. Biking out of Glacier National Park you can see the mountains meet the flat horizon as you enter the plains. It is here where the land dries and the trees shrink to shrubs. Wind is no longer howling across lakes or up mountain faces, but instead it stirs dirt and highway debris.

WHAT STATE HAD THE MOST DIFFICULT TERRAIN?

One might think that Washington is the most difficult, as it is chock full of mountain passes. However, to the conditioned cyclist, they pale in comparison to the rolling valleys of Pennsylvania. I would much rather climb one pass all day than 5 valley climbs by lunch.

WHAT WAS THE BIGGEST DANGER YOU FACED?

RV's, dogs, and drivers that don't pay attention. RV drivers, in my opinion, are more dangerous than logging trucks! I always felt safer when a logging truck went past me because I know that the drivers have a serious set of skills that enable them to drive the trucks with great precision. RV's on the other hand, made me nervous because I couldn't help but think that just a week ago the driver's had never driven something so big in their life! Plus, the mirrors are the size of a refrigerator, inching their way into the shoulder of the road.

Dogs never got me into trouble, but they got my heart rate going more than once. It is more than likely that you will encounter a dog or two that will chase you down with all it's might, snarling at your ankles as you pedal like mad. In Montana, I had to bike 26 miles an hour uphill to escape a feral dog that was trying to eat my ankles for lunch. Terrifying? A little bit.

WHAT WAS YOUR LONGEST MILEAGE DAY? SHORTEST?

In North Dakota I biked 136 miles in a day, which was my longest day only by about 12 miles. My shortest day was the first day of my trip, where I biked 30 miles, from Port Townsend, Washington to Deception Pass, Washington. This was essentially my introduction to biking on the shoulder of a busy road.

WHAT WAS YOUR AVERAGE DAILY MILES?

I spent about seven hours a day, averaging 90 miles—which comes out to about 13 miles an hour. Pretty neat, huh? You don't have to haul ass to get across the country!

WHAT WAS YOUR EXACT ROUTE?

Towns in **Bold** *have hostels that I stayed at. I have listed the hostels on P. 62.*

1. Port Townsend to Deception Pass, WA
2. Deception Pass, WA to Hamilton, WA
3. Hamilton, WA to Newhalem, WA
4. Newhalem, WA to **Winthrop, WA**

5. Winthrop, WA to Riverside, WA
6. Riverside, WA to Republic, WA
7. Republic, WA to **Colville, WA**
8. Bacon Bike hostel to Ione, WA
9. Ione, WA to Sandpoint, ID
10. Sandpoint, ID to Kalispell, MT
11. Kalispell, MT to West Glacier, MT
12. West Glacier, MT to **East Glacier, MT**
13. The Backpacker's Inn to Shelby, MT
14. Shelby, MT to Havre, MT
15. Havre, MT to Malta, MT
16. Malta, MT to Wolf Point, MT
17. Wolf Point, MT to Glendive, MT
18. Glendive, MT to Medrona, MT
19. Medrona, MT to Hebron, MT
20. Hebron, MT to Bismark, ND
21. Bismark, ND to **Gackle, ND**
22. The Honey Hostel, to Barnesville, MN
23. Barnesville, MN to Alexandria, MN
24. Alexandria, MN to Monticello, MN
25. Monticello, MN to St. Paul, MN
26. St. Paul, MN to Alma, WI
27. Alma, WI to Coon Valley, WI
28. Coon Valley, WI to Spring Green, WI
29. Spring Green, WI to Madison, WI
30. Madison, WI to Milwuakee, WI
31. Milwuakee, WI to Grand Haven, MI
32. Grand Haven, MI to Lansing, MI
33. Lansing, MI to Adrian, MI
34. Adrian, MI to Clyde, OH
35. Clyde, OH to Akron, OH
36. Akron, OH to Chardon, OH
37. Chardon, OH to Meadville, PA
38. Meadville, PA to Ludlow, PA
39. Ludlow, PA to Coudersport, PA

40. Coudersport, PA to Troy, PA
41. Troy, PA to Elmhurst, PA
42. Elmhurst, PA to Gardiner, NY
43. Gardiner, NY to Beacon Falls, CT
44. Beacon Falls, CT to Noank, CT
45. Noank, CT to Rochester, MA
46. Rochester, MA to Vineyard Haven, MA

WHAT ABOUT PUBLIC LANDS?

PUBLIC LANDS AND NATIONAL PARKS

I love the outdoors. There is nothing that makes me feel more at home than fresh air and wilderness. As an American, I am proud and humbled to have access to roughly 640 million acres of public land. Stretching from mountain peaks to river valleys, open plains to dense forests, this land is part of who we are. It is my wish that everyone gets to experience the joy of our country's rich landscape.

Unfortunately, not everyone shares that wish. Today, our government and private interests alike are rallying day and night to eliminate public lands and sell off acres for short term energy solutions and profit, at the expense of the planet and without our consent. The very places we flock to when we need peace and quiet, solitude and vastness are on the brink of destruction.

Whether you are a hiker, skier, biker, camper, kayaker, fly-fisher, canoer, barefoot walker or animal stalker this affects you! However, this is an issue that not only affects us humans; it affects the animals that live here, the fish in our rivers, and the health of our planet. We are their voice too! So, what can we do as individuals to ensure that land stays in public domain and we can continue to enjoy our places of solitude and recreation?

We can stay informed and involved! This can be as simple as calling your State Representative and voicing your concern, or getting behind an organization to support the political fight for our public land.

Did you know that by simply purchasing this book you have already helped make an impact? That's right! I am donating $1.00 from every book purchased directly to the Outdoor Alliance®.

On the next page, I have listed multiple organizations that have been fighting to protect our public lands. Check them out on the next page!

Each organization listed is a 501(c)3 nonprofit.

The Access Fund
www.accessfund.org
Outdoor Alliance
www.outdooralliance.org
American Canoe Association
www.americancanoe.org
American Whitewater
www.americanwhitewater.org
International Mountain Biking Association
www.imba.org
Winter Wildlands Alliance
www.winterwildlands.org
The Mountaineers
www.themountaineers.org
The American Alpine Club
www.americanalpineclub.org
The Trust for Public Land
www.tpl.org
Keep It Public
www.keepitpublic.org

RESOURCES & F.A.Q.

A FEW PHOTOS

Day one of my trip, no idea what I was getting myself into. Oak Harbor, WA

Ah, the graded hill sign... Somewhere in Washington.

I took this same photo at every state line sign.

RESOURCES & F.A.Q.

Picking up a general delivery package, "Please hold for cyclist".

A typical Bike round-up at a hotel in Montana.

Camping in a backyard in St. Paul, Minnesota.

Attack of a near-fatal flat tire. Out of tubes and in the middle of Ohio. I ended up hitching a ride into the nearest town with a bike shop, 70 miles away.

RESOURCES & F.A.Q.

Discovering the joy of over-packing, in Wisconsin. I mailed my rain pants home too... Bad idea.

Totally wiped out, eating lunch at a grocery store in Montana.

Taking a selfie at the Continental Divide. Rainstorms ensued.

Camp is where you park it! Hebron, Montana.

RESOURCES & F.A.Q.

Hugging my dad with an unexpected group of friends and family. Unreal!

Dipping my front tire in the Atlantic ocean, trip complete! Martha's Vineyard, Massachusetts, August 6th 2014.

THANK YOU!

Thank you for reading my book, and please reach out to me if you decide to ride across the United States.
I would love to hear about your trip!

youcanbikeacrossamerica@gmail.com

RESOURCES & F.A.Q.

MORE ABOUT THE AUTHOR

Isaiah is never done learning, never done seeking.

Portrait by Jules Smith Photography®

Made in the USA
Columbia, SC
24 September 2020